CGP

TRUE STORIES

&

UEENS

Credits

Editors: Claire Boulter, Holly Poynton

Consultant: Rachel Clark

Reviewers: Judith Hornigold, Alison Griffin

With thanks to Paul Jordin, Anthony Muller, Rebecca Tate, Samantha Bensted, Janet Berkeley, Amanda MacNaughton and Maxine Petrie for the proofreading.

With thanks to Laura Jakubowski for the copyright research.

With thanks to John Kitching for the design work.

Published by CGP

ISBN: 978 1 84762 474 1

Printed by Elanders Ltd, Newcastle upon Tyne.

The chapters in this book are based on real people and real events. However, some situations and dialogue have been changed for dramatic purposes. Some minor characters have been invented; any similarity to a real person, living or dead, is purely coincidence.

Contents

Acknowledgements

Boadicea image on cover and introduction page © Look and Learn

Background image on cover © iStockphoto.com/duncan1890

Boadicea image on contents page and page 9: Private Collection © Look and Learn / Bridgeman Images

Image on page 2: Family life in the Iron Age. Private Collection / © English Heritage Photo Library / Bridgeman Images

Image on page 4: Typical London Street in Roman Times. Private Collection © Look and Learn / Bridgeman Images

Image on page 7: The scourging of Boadicea. Private Collection / The Stapleton Collection / Bridgeman Images

Image on page 10: Aerial View of Roman London. Private Collection © Look and Learn / Bridgeman Images

Image on page 15: England Great Army Map © Hel-hama, licensed for re-use under the creative commons licence, http://creativecommons.org/licenses/by-sa/3.0/deed.en

Image on page 16: Viking and longship. Private Collection © Look and Learn / Bridgeman Images

Image on page 28: Fontevraud abbey cloister (photo). Godong / UIG / Bridgeman Images

Image on page 42: Victoria Regina, 1887. Royal Collection Trust © Her Majesty Queen Elizabeth II, 2014 / Bridgeman Images

Image on page 43: Queen Victoria receiving the Sacrament at her Coronation. Royal Collection Trust © Her Majesty Queen Elizabeth II, 2014 / Bridgeman Images

Image on page 44: Queen Victoria, 1847. Royal Collection Trust © Her Majesty Queen Elizabeth II, 2014 / Bridgeman Images

Image on page 46: The Opening of the Great Exhibition. Private Collection / Bridgeman Images

Image on page 50: The Queen presenting a jubilee mug to Miss Florence Dunn (engraving). Private Collection © Look and Learn / Peter Jackson Collection / Bridgeman Images

Image on page 51: Queen Victoria, Empress of India and Abdul Karim 'The Munshi'. The Illustrated London News Picture Library, London, UK / Bridgeman Images

Image on page 52: Queen Victoria's (1819-1901) Imperial state crown. © Museum of London, UK / Bridgeman Images

With thanks to Alamy, CGTextures.com, Clipart.com, iStockphoto.com and Thinkstockphotos.co.uk for permission to use the stock images in this book.

Boudica

"The warrior queen"

written by Holly Poynton

OCTOBER 42 AD Boudica (Boo-dik-a) ducked. The sword sliced at the air above her head, and whistled past her tawny hair. She had to think fast. Pulling the hidden dagger from inside her boot, she thrust it at her attacker's shoe.

"Ow! That hurt! We're only meant to be practising, Boudica. No need to chop my foot off!" her assailant exclaimed, as he dropped his own wooden sword to nurse his big toe. Boudica stood up, and patted Aiden on the back. Even though she was two years younger than her tribesman, she towered over him.

Boudica was only twelve, but she already had a reputation as a fierce warrior. None of the other children at warrior school liked to practise with her; they always came away with bruises and scratches when they did. Only Aiden was brave enough to face her.

Boudica may have belonged to the Iceni (eye-seen-eye) tribe. This tribe lived in an area of south-eastern Britain, in and around modern-day Norfolk. The Iceni people were divided into lots of smaller groups called clans.

Boudica had lived with Aiden and his family since her eighth winter, so he was a brother to her in every way except blood. As was tradition, Boudica's mother had placed her in the care of Aiden's family to strengthen the relationship between the two clans.

Although Boudica's life here was a full and happy one, she would occasionally sneak out of the roundhouse at night to gaze at the sky. She would stare at the inky blackness above, hoping that her mother was looking up at the same stars and thinking of her.

The Iceni people lived in roundhouses.

1

The Calm Before the Storm

AIDEN JABBED BOUDICA in her ribs with the tip of his sword. "Stop day-dreaming, silly." Boudica snapped back to reality and swung her own sword at Aiden's shins in retaliation. "Right! This means war!" yelled Aiden. Boudica took off through a wheat field, Aiden close behind her.

As the maze of crops thinned out, they saw their roundhouse across the next field, the smoke from that evening's cooking fire seeping through the thatched roof.

"Last one home has to feed the pigs!" hollered Boudica as she drew on her last ounce of energy and surged towards home. She willed her legs to go faster, but Aiden easily overtook her, slapping his palm on the wattle and daub wall first.

Aiden's mother heard the commotion, and poked her head out of the door just as Boudica reached the house, panting heavily.

Wattle was made by weaving twigs and branches through wooden stakes. Daub was a wet mixture made from clay, earth, sand, water and straw. It was applied to the wattle and left to dry and harden.

"Where have you two been? You were supposed to help me cook dinner!" Aiden's mother exclaimed. She plucked at Aiden's cloak, "Have you been running through the muddy fields again?" Aiden's brightly coloured, woollen cloak and tunic were splattered in dirt, and Boudica's leather boots were caked in mud. "Honestly! Go and tell your father that dinner's almost ready, he's harvesting crops in the next field." Aiden's mother went back to the fire and turned the spit, the scent of roasted pork filling the roundhouse.

"Race you to the field?" whispered Boudica. "Loser has to feed the pigs."

This is what the inside of a roundhouse may have looked like.

A Powerful Enemy

43 AD Boudica leapt from the thicket, her bowstring taut. But, instead of the deer she expected to see, she found herself face to face with a Roman messenger. The unarmed boy took one look at the imposing British archer, dropped his satchel of letters and sped off into the forest. Curious, Boudica picked a letter out of the bag and began to read.

Dearest Mother,   *August 23rd, 43 AD*

So much has happened since my last letter! Earlier this year, our noble Emperor, Claudius, ordered us to invade Britannia. I, along with 40,000 other Roman soldiers, packed up my belongings and set sail across the sea. I was quite nervous about arriving in Britannia; I had heard tales about the savage Britons and their bloodthirsty ways.

When we landed in Britannia, we weren't met with a warm welcome! One of the British tribes, the Catuvellauni (Kay-too-vel-arni), had amassed an army in the hope of driving us out. The barbarians positioned themselves on the western side of a wide river, and lined 150,000 men along the bank. Seeing that line of fearsome warriors stretched out in front of us was quite intimidating, but we held our ground.

The following day, our army launched an attack. Although we were far better disciplined and equipped, the battle still lasted for two days. The sheer number of Britons made them a formidable opponent, and many of them fought without armour, so they were quick and nimble. Some of their warriors even paint their bodies blue before battle, which makes them seem terrifying and wild.

On the second day, the Catuvellauni started to retreat, and we knew we'd defeated them. Once the other British tribes saw how easily we'd dispatched one of their largest and most powerful tribes, the other tribal kings were quick to bend the knee to Rome! Already the Brigantes (Bree-gan-tees), Atrebates (A-treb-ay-tees) and Iceni have surrendered.

I am currently living in a place called Camulodunon (Cam-ul-o-dun-on). It used to be an important British town, but we've demolished their dirty roundhouses and started building some beautiful stone temples and villas. The Britons are fairly uncivilised, but once they've experienced Roman culture I'm sure they'll be converted to our sophisticated way of life.

The socks you sent are gratefully received. I'll write again when I have more news.

Your loving son,

An Uneasy Peace

JUNE 55 AD Boudica gazed at her husband, Prasutagus (Pra-soo-tag-us), as he sat by the cooking fire, his noble profile casting a shadow across the walls of their roundhouse. He was the leader of the Iceni people and a **client king** to Rome.

Life had changed very little for the Iceni tribe since the invasion, but Boudica knew that Camulodunon (modern-day Colchester), the former capital of the Trinovante (Try-no-van-tee) tribe, had changed dramatically. The town was now the largest Roman settlement in Britain and was home to 3000 **veteran** soldiers. Boudica had heard rumours about the strange customs of these invaders, and she longed to see the town for herself.

Prasutagus frequently travelled to Camulodunon to meet with Roman officials, and after much begging from Boudica, he finally relented and let her accompany him.

JULY 55 AD As they entered the town, Boudica stared at the buildings, open-mouthed. The traditional roundhouses were gone, and in their place stood row upon row of stone structures. Prasutagus clasped her hand excitedly and began pointing out some of the unfamiliar buildings.

"Over there are the public baths, where people go to wash. Further up that street is the theatre; it's absolutely huge and it can hold thousands of people. Every month they put on amazing performances for people to go and see. It certainly beats gathering round the fire listening to the village elders telling stories!" Prasutagus stopped and pointed proudly to a half-finished building, larger than any Boudica had seen before. "They are building a temple to honour the dead emperor, Claudius. Isn't it magnificent? It makes our **sacred groves** look a bit pathetic really!"

This picture shows what Camulodunon might have looked like.

Camulodunon Courier

Monday, July 28 55 AD   ONE COIN

ROME: FRIEND OR FOE?

Special Report

SINCE THE ROMAN invasion more than ten years ago, Camulodunon residents have experienced great upheaval — but have these Roman invaders improved or worsened life for locals? On the one hand, the Romans brought us clean water, better health, more money and new leisure activities. On the other hand, they have enslaved us, taxed us and taken away our weapons. Is this a fair deal for Camulodunon? The *Courier* investigates.

Clean water — at a cost

One of the first things the Romans did when they arrived was build an aqueduct to deliver fresh water into the heart of Camulodunon. Thanks to a constant supply of clean water, local residents have suffered very few outbreaks of sickness. But this improvement in our health has come at a price: the aqueduct was built by enslaved Britons, many of whom suffered injury or death during the process.

A taxing invasion?

Since the invasion, British merchants have been able to take advantage of Roman trade routes to sell their goods much further afield for a higher price. As a result, some traders in Camulodunon have become very rich. However, Rome now demands high taxes from everyone in Camulodunon. For rich merchants, these taxes are annoying, but poorer British families are left with barely enough money to scrape by.

A double-edged sword?

There's no doubt that the Romans have introduced Britons to some exotic and luxurious pastimes (visits to bath houses, theatres and chariot races are just a few examples), but Rome seems intent on stamping out traditional British activities. Non-Romans have been banned from carrying weapons, so they can no longer enjoy weapons practice or swordplay. One disgruntled resident, whose axe was confiscated last week, claimed "Them Romans don't want us Britons practisin', cos they know we'll be harder to control if we're well-trained."

A better Britain?

Locals are divided about whether Rome has had a positive or negative effect overall. Are we better off under the Roman rule? Only time will tell.

A Servant of Rome

57 AD Boudica's daughters sat cross-legged on the floor, watching their father intently. Their bright little faces crinkled with laughter as he acted out a traditional Iceni tale about a brave warrior and a cunning wolf. Occasionally, he would wrap a **pelt** around his shoulders and crawl across the floor, snapping playfully at their bare toes.

Boudica had heard this tale countless times from her own father who, in turn, had heard it from his father. Boudica wondered whether in another fifty years anyone would remember this story at all. Since the Romans had invaded, more and more traditions and beliefs were vanishing.

Boudica knew it was sensible to be allied with Rome: client kingdoms were safe from the Roman army and were given protection from enemy tribes. But recently, she felt as though the Roman presence was casting an ominous shadow over her country, and the knot in her stomach grew tighter day by day.

A replica Roman helmet

60 AD Boudica knelt at her husband's bedside, clutching his fevered hand in hers. She felt the hot tears stream uncontrollably down her face.

Although Prasutagus was given the title of king, he only ruled a small part of Britain; there were many other Celtic kings at this time. Celtic kings were more like elected chiefs rather than the kings and queens we have today.

"My wife," King Prasutagus began, his breathing raspy. "Half of my kingdom is now yours to rule. Look after it for our daughters and our people." Boudica shook her head, halfheartedly.

"You have many years ahead of you yet, my husband. You will soon…"

Prasutagus interrupted her. "My time has come, Boudica. You are a good queen. Promise me you will be a strong and just ruler."

Boudica made her promise to Prasutagus, but he could no longer hear her.

6

The Beginning of the End

MAY 60 AD It had been several weeks since Prasutagus had died, and it seemed that any hope of a peaceful coexistence with Rome had died along with him.

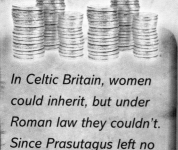

In Celtic Britain, women could inherit, but under Roman law they couldn't. Since Prasutagus left no male heirs, his kingdom came under Roman rule.

Boudica clenched her fists. Not content with what they had already stolen from Britain, Rome was now demanding that she step down as queen and hand over full control of the Iceni lands and people to them. For too long she had tolerated these Roman vultures as they pecked at the bones of her country. She felt the old warrior spirit within her unfurl. She would defy Rome for the sake of her daughters! She would not let these invaders snatch away her children's birthright!

JUNE 60 AD Boudica heard the whip slap through the air before she felt the lash sting her back. Was that the sixteenth or seventeenth strike? The skin on her back was raw. Every breath she took sent a searing pain through the wounds. She bit her lip and refused to cry out; she couldn't appear weak in front of her Roman torturers.

Blindfolded, Boudica's senses were heightened. She heard a familiar cry. Then a piercing scream. Her daughters! Not content with punishing her, the Romans had targeted her daughters too. They were still children, just ten and twelve years old.

Boudica thrashed and howled, desperately trying to free herself from the **fetters** they had clamped around her legs. She needed to protect her children, but the chains that held her were too strong. All she could do was weep and listen helplessly.

A painting which shows what Boudica's punishment may have been like.

7

A Warrior's Plea

JULY 60 AD Boudica stood before the 100 000-strong crowd who had gathered to hear her speak. News of her brutal flogging and the abuse her daughters had faced at the hands of the Romans had spread quickly amongst the Celtic people. Men, women and children had travelled from miles around to show their solidarity and hear what the Iceni queen had to say. She wasn't nervous or afraid; she knew that her cause was just. She was going to seek revenge for what the Romans had done to her in the only way she knew how: with her sword.

My fellow clansmen, I stand before you, not as your queen but as an Iceni woman. An Iceni woman whose daughters were tormented by these Roman brutes! An Iceni woman who was cruelly beaten for defending what was rightfully hers! An Iceni woman who wants to put an end to the Roman stranglehold which is choking our country.

Who amongst you have faced injustice at the hands of the Romans? Who amongst you have lost loved ones at the hands of these brutes? Our fellow clansmen are captured and forced into slavery. Plucked from their homes and beaten and whipped into obedience, they are forced to bow down to these pathetic dogs.

I look at the faces before me, and I see noble British tribes. The proud Iceni! The brave Trinovantes! Unless we act now, I will no longer see the faces of my clansmen around me. I will see Roman faces. Roman faces who have destroyed our heritage and culture. They came to Britain and they took our land. I say that it is time we took it back!

Even if none of you join me in battle, I will fight alone. For it is better to fight as a free Briton, than to live in peace as a Roman slave.

But if you have been wronged by the Romans, fight alongside me. If you fear the Romans will destroy our culture, add your sword to mine. The Romans think we are weak. Let us show them that we are a force to be reckoned with. We will march on Camulodunon and kill all the Romans we find. We will show these invaders that we are not sheep, we are wolves! We are fierce and brave! We are Britons!

© Mary Evans Picture Library / Alamy

A City in Flames

BOUDICA'S HEART THUMPED IN HER CHEST. She had her army, but now she needed to know if the gods were on her side. Thousands of people were gathered around her, but their silence roared in her ears. A local chief passed her the hare, and its velvety body squirmed and wriggled in her trembling hands.

This ancient ritual was vitally important in predicting the future: if the hare ran to the left, her army would face almost certain defeat, but if the hare ran to the right, victory would be theirs. With a deep breath, she took the frantic animal by the scruff of the neck and wrapped it in the material of her skirt. She muttered a prayer to the gods and opened the folds of her skirt. The hare sprang forwards and into the undergrowth.

Was that the silence roaring in her ears still? No! That was the sound of 100 000 voices crashing over her like a waterfall! The hare had leapt to the right! The gods were on their side. They would be victorious!

BOUDICA WIPED THE BLOOD AND SOOT FROM THE EDGE OF HER SPEAR.
Camulodunon lay behind her in ruins. Her army had easily ransacked the town; only 2000 Roman soldiers had opposed her, and they had merely been old men.

As her army had rushed through the city streets, killing or burning everyone and everything that stood before them, the Roman civilians had fled like ships before a storm and barricaded themselves in the temple of Claudius.

Boudica had once been awed by the magnificent temple, but now it represented everything she despised. When the flames finally took hold of the structure, she watched for hours as it disintegrated into a pile of smouldering rubble.

Boudica leads her army into battle.

The Unstoppable Tide

BOUDICA SURVEYED HER NEXT TARGET COOLLY: Londinium (modern-day London). The town had been built rapidly over the past fifteen years, and the Romans had paid little attention to protecting it from attack. Like Camulodunon, it was unwalled, so entry into the city would be easy. There were few Roman soldiers in the vicinity and those Romans that did remain were fat merchants who would be no match for thousands of Celtic warriors. Boudica sharpened her blade and waited.

THREE DAYS LATER Boudica and her army were marching towards Verulamium (Ver-oo-lay-mee-um) (modern-day St Albans). Much like Camulodunon, Londinium had fallen easily. Boudica had barely slept since their victory in Camulodunon; her hair was matted with blood and her face was streaked with soot. Her blue eyes were wild, and her right hand never strayed from the shaft of her spear.

Aiden, her old childhood friend, rode by her side, his brow knotted. "Verulamium is home to Britons, Boudica. The land has belonged to the Catuvellauni tribe for generations. Can we destroy our fellow countrymen?"

Boudica turned away from Aiden and stared ahead. "Perhaps once they were Britons, but the Catuvellauni are Roman puppets now. They welcomed these brutes into their town, and they have shunned Celtic traditions. If they do not side with us, then they are our enemy, Aiden. Verulamium will burn, and it will burn tomorrow!"

This image gives an idea of what Londinium might have looked like. It was much smaller than modern-day London.

The Battle for Britain

THE EVENING WAS DRAWING IN, and Boudica wrapped her furs about her more tightly. Camulodunon, Londinium and Verulamium had all been destroyed. Tomorrow, her army would face the forces of the Roman leader, Suetonius (Sway-tony-us).

This foe would be different from the ones they had previously faced; Suetonius was an experienced military leader with a highly disciplined army. If her army could defeat Suetonius's forces, Boudica hoped that the Roman army would be broken, and the remaining Romans would withdraw from Britain.

Boudica could just about make out the enemy encampment nestled between two hills. She watched as the Roman soldiers scurried about like ants, putting up flimsy little tents and gathering kindling, the fading light glinting off their polished armour.

*Suetonius and his army had been fighting the **druids** on the Island of Mona (modern day Anglesey) when Boudica's rebellion begun. When it became clear that Boudica posed a real threat to Rome's rule, his army was sent to end the uprising once and for all.*

Boudica turned and surveyed her own people, small groups huddled by the thousands of campfires that glittered for miles around. Unlike the enemy, her army looked powerful and strong. They didn't need the armour or the weapons the Romans put their faith in. She felt confident. So confident in fact, that she had let Suetonius choose where he positioned his army. The gods were on her side, her army outnumbered the Roman forces twenty-to-one and her people were fighting for their homeland. Victory would surely be hers.

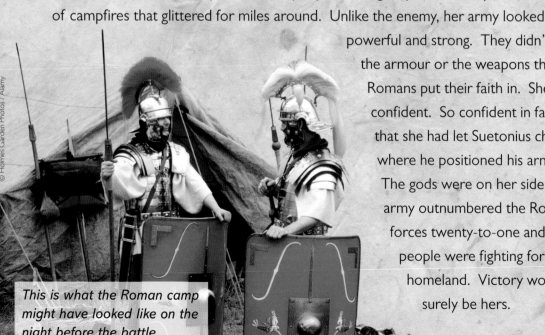

This is what the Roman camp might have looked like on the night before the battle.

© Holmes Garden Photos / Alamy

A Field Painted in Blood

Hail our great and glorious Emperor!

What follows is a battle report. It explains how Suetonius and his forces dealt with the British uprising.

1. *The battle site that Suetonius chose was of strategic importance:*

    - *He selected an area with a wood behind him. This ensured that the enemy forces could not attack him from behind.*

    - *He chose a narrow stretch of land in a valley. Thus the flanks of his army were protected on either side by high ground.*

    - *The narrow entrance also meant that the rebels were forced into a bottleneck — fewer Britons were able to attack at once. Consequently, the size of their army counted for nothing.*

    - *Suetonius's forces were positioned on higher ground. Therefore the rebel army was disadvantaged by attacking uphill.*

2. *The Roman forces were dressed for battle in full armour. The British forces were poorly prepared and many went into battle without armour.*

3. *Although the rebel army outnumbered the Roman forces, the discipline and the training of the Roman army quickly vanquished the Britons. The rebel army was made up of women, children and untrained men.*

4. *The rebels had left thousands of carts containing their possessions close to their army. Once the Britons realised they had lost and tried to retreat, these carts got in the way of them escaping.*

Suetonius advises that the remaining Britons from the rebel tribes are punished to set an example. Only by demonstrating Rome's might can we be sure that an uprising of this scale will not happen again.

Marcus

A Peaceful End

BOUDICA HAD LOST EVERYTHING: her army, her daughters, her country. She cradled the bodies of her children as she hummed a traditional Iceni lullaby. With trembling fingers, she rubbed a smear of dirt from her youngest daughter's pale, cold cheek.

Records disagree about the cause of Boudica's death. One source says she poisoned herself and her daughters, whereas another says that she succumbed to a fatal illness and was given an impressive funeral.

Boudica had fled the battlefield when she had realised the battle was unwinnable. Soon the Romans would discover that she was not among the dead, and then they would scour the surrounding hills and hunt her down like a dog. Nestled in a secluded grove of trees, Boudica knew they would find her eventually, but she wouldn't give them the satisfaction of taking her alive. She would die now, on her terms. It wouldn't be a warrior's death, but she would breathe her last with her feet on British soil and her daughters by her side.

Boudica crushed the **hemlock** leaves in her fist and put them in her mouth. She wrapped her arms around her daughters, closed her eyes and prayed for sleep.

Glossary

client king — A ruler that kept his lands, on the understanding that he would obey the demands of another, more important, ruler

druids — Holy men and women who knew about religion, medicine and the law. The druids were a very important group of people in British society

fetters — Restraints put around the feet

hemlock — A highly poisonous plant

pelt — The skin of an animal with the fur or hair still on it

sacred groves — Forests that were of religious importance to Celtic tribes

veteran — A long-serving or retired soldier

Alfred the Great

"The first King of England"

written by Claire Boulter

OCTOBER 1849 The mouth-watering scent of roasted ox filled the chilly autumn air as the children pushed their way through the crowd. They had never seen the streets of Wantage, the sleepy market town where they lived, so full of people. The town was a riot of colour — flags and banners hung from every window and lamppost, and fragrant flowers were strewn across the roads.

Everywhere the children looked, some new attraction caught their eye — stalls selling sweet roasted chestnuts and bags of golden toffee; a striped tent housing a fortune teller; a carousel on which graceful horses leapt and whirled.

Reaching the front of the crowd, the children could just glimpse a procession of people making their way along the road towards them. Their voices rose in song, louder than the chatter and laughter all around.

> **"Today is the day of a thousand years!**
> **Bless it, O brothers, with heart-thrilling cheers!**
> **Alfred for ever! – today was he born,**
> **Day-star of England, to herald her morn"**

The oldest child nudged his best friend with his elbow and laughed. "Just think, Davey — they've gone to all this effort just to celebrate some old king who was born a thousand years ago! He must have been really important."

This statue of King Alfred was erected in Wantage in 1877. It was unveiled by the Prince and Princess of Wales.

The 1849 jubilee was one of many celebrations of Alfred's life. An even bigger event was held in Winchester in 1901 to remember his death.

An Unpromising Start

OCTOBER 849 With a deft movement, the midwife wrapped the newborn baby in a piece of cloth and laid him gently in his mother's arms.

"Another son for you, my lady," the old woman croaked. Queen Osburh (Oz-bur) stroked the small, crumpled face with one finger and softly kissed the thatch of red-blond hair.

"Alfred," she murmured as the midwife left the room. Outside the door, the midwife frowned to herself. Another boy was all well and good, but with four older brothers in line for the throne, Alfred was hardly going to change history, was he?

In the ninth century England was made up of four kingdoms, each with its own ruler. Alfred's family ruled Wessex. Each kingdom was divided into shires (counties).

APRIL 871 Alfred sighed and wiped a hand across his eyes. Placing his brother's sword upon his lifeless chest, he stepped back and watched as the stone was lowered over Ethelred's (Eth-ull-red's) tomb.

One by one, Alfred had buried his mother, his father and his four brothers. The latest loss was the hardest: Ethelred was only a few years older than Alfred, and the two had grown up together. They had fought side by side against the Viking invaders who terrorised the land. Alfred had watched in horror as the Viking axe that would end Ethelred's life had swung in a glittering arc, bright against the steel sky.

Forcing the image from his mind, Alfred lifted his chin and met the eyes of the assembled noblemen. He couldn't bring his family back, but as king he would fight for the land they had loved.

A map showing the kingdoms of England in the ninth century.

15

Danger from the North

TWO MONTHS LATER Alfred held his breath as he gazed across the table at the Viking King, Guthrum (Guth-rum). Alfred's army had fought Guthrum's and lost. Now, Alfred's only hope was that Guthrum would agree to a **peace treaty**. In exchange for the Vikings leaving Wessex, Alfred had offered them a huge sum of money. He knew it wasn't a popular decision with his noblemen, who would have to foot the bill. He also knew that it was his only chance to save his kingdom.

Guthrum narrowed his eyes as one of his advisors bent down and whispered in his ear. Then, with a nod, he stood and shook Alfred's hand. The deal was struck. Wessex was safe.

Most Vikings came from Scandinavian countries like Denmark and Norway. They settled in many places, including Britain, France, Iceland and Greenland.

15th June 871
Price ½ d

The Dorchester Herald

SPECIAL EDITION

THE VIKINGS — MONSTERS OR MEN?

Ask most people about the Vikings, and chances are they'll have a story to tell — how their village was raided; how their crops were burned and their cattle stolen; how they saw their church destroyed by bearded thugs wearing horned helmets.

But how much truth lies behind these stories? Are the Vikings really bloodthirsty killers intent on destruction, or just normal men struggling to find their place in the world? I spent a month undercover in a Viking village to learn the facts behind the rumours.

Rumour 1 — All Vikings do is plunder
The Vikings have a reputation for raiding villages and living off what they steal. However, I learnt that only a small number of men go on raids — most are occupied with farming, building boats and making

A typical Viking? Perhaps not.

weapons. In fact, their lives are much like ours.

Rumour 2 — Vikings are dirty and unkempt
Like most people, I always thought Vikings were filthy, with long, unwashed hair

and beards. Imagine my surprise on finding out that they bathe every Saturday! This is shockingly frequent compared to our own annual baths. The Vikings also own combs made of bone, and comb their hair and beard daily.

Rumour 3 — Vikings wear horned helmets

Every **Anglo-Saxon** child hears stories of burly Vikings wearing horned helmets who will steal them away if they're naughty. During my time with the Vikings I didn't see so much as a single horn. Viking helmets are simple bowl shapes made from iron, with a guard to protect the nose. In fact, a Viking woman told me that the myth of the horned helmet was dreamt up by an Anglo-Saxon bishop, to make the Vikings seem more barbaric!

Rumour 4 — Vikings are demons

There are many reports of Viking warriors going crazy during battle — howling like wolves and biting their shields. Many people believe that they are devils who can't be harmed by any man. However, one Viking warrior revealed how a normally calm man can enter a trance where he has no fear or knowledge of what he is doing. They call the warriors who do this 'berserkers'.

I have to conclude that, although they seem fearsome, Vikings really aren't so different from you and me.

JANUARY 878 Alfred leaned back in his chair and sighed contentedly. It had been a wonderful Christmas, packed with music, plays and fine food. Tonight, **Twelfth Night**, was the high point of the celebrations — Alfred had exchanged gifts with his friends and enjoyed a wonderful feast. He yawned and stretched luxuriously.

Suddenly, there was a shout from outside and the clash of swords. Alfred leapt to his feet. A guard burst in, blood pouring from a wound to his shoulder.

"Sire," he yelled, "the Vikings are here! We are heavily outnumbered. You must flee." Alfred looked from one door to the other — behind the first, the attackers; behind the second, safety. A hand gripped his arm, pulling him towards the second door. With a cry, he gave in and sped out into the protecting night.

The Lonely King

ALFRED RAN FOR HOURS. His ragged breath tore at his throat, and his legs felt like lead weights. But the greatest pain was in his heart — the knowledge that the Vikings had taken control of Wessex, and he had let his subjects down.

Beside him ran his bodyguard, a small handful of hardened warriors. They were tough, he knew, but not tough enough to fend off another Viking attack. As he ran, Alfred racked his brain, desperately trying to come up with a plan to defeat the invaders. As the blood-red sun crept above the horizon, Alfred finally accepted that he couldn't fight — he had to find somewhere to hide, to buy himself time.

One night, Alfred rested in the hut of a peasant woman. Not knowing he was King, she asked him to watch the bread she was baking, to make sure it didn't burn. Deep in thought, Alfred let the bread burn and was scolded. Alfred realised his kingdom was like the bread — he had to look after it to make it succeed.

MARCH 878 Perched on the slope of the small, conical hill, Alfred scanned the land all around him, alert for any movement. Save for the wheeling flight of a kestrel high above, all was still, and Alfred felt himself relax for the first time since the attack.

The past two months had been the hardest of his life. With his small band of loyal men, he had trudged through mile after mile of treacherous marsh, searching for a safe place to stop, a place where Guthrum couldn't find him. Now, at last, he had found it. At last, he could start to recover his strength, to plan, to gather an army, to fight for Wessex.

The small hill where Alfred ended up was Burrow Mump in Somerset. At the time, it was surrounded by marsh, but this was drained in the 13th century.

© Photos.com/Thinkstock

SEVEN WEEKS LATER Alfred rode east, his mind a storm of hope and fear. From his base at Burrow Mump, he had sent out messengers to summon all the men they could find, to form an army and fight the Vikings. Now he was riding to meet his new army, but he had no idea whether he had any support left in Wessex, whether anyone would respond to his call.

Emerging from a gloomy forest into a wide, flower-strewn meadow, Alfred squinted in the sudden brightness. As his eyes adjusted, he saw, ranged in front of him, thousands of armed men. A great cheer went up from the assembled army — they were ready to fight for him.

In Alfred's time, each shire (county) had a small army called a fyrd (furd) that could be called on to defend the kingdom when needed. Many of the men in each fyrd were farmers — they had to leave their farms to fight.

4ᵗʰ May 878, late evening

What an exciting day! The rumour that the king is alive and plans to fight the Vikings is true! For weeks that's all that anyone has talked about, but we hardly dared to believe it. Today I, an ordinary blacksmith, have seen the great man himself.

The Vikings have been a threat for as long as I can remember, but with King Alfred gone it was obvious that the Viking villain, Guthrum, planned to conquer the whole of Wessex. Every day we heard of a raid on another village, and we lived in constant fear.

We set off early this morning. Arriving at the meeting place at noon, we found dozens of men already there. The buzz of conversation filled the air, and everyone was laughing and joking in a way that they hadn't for months. As the day drew on, more and more men arrived — a great army that stretched as far as the eye could see.

I was chatting to Osgar, when all at once a hush fell upon the crowd. Looking around, I saw him, King Alfred himself! His eyes filled with tears when he saw us, and as one we began to cheer, banging our weapons on our shields to show our support.

Then Alfred spoke, for all to hear. He described a great war against the Vikings, driving them from Wessex once and for all. He spoke so passionately that we would have followed him anywhere. So, tomorrow we march to war, for Wessex and for glory!

A New Dawn

JUST FORTY-EIGHT HOURS HAD PASSED, but to Alfred it seemed like a lifetime. He had fought the Vikings and won — even as he repeated the words to himself he could hardly believe it.

The battle had raged fiercely for many hours, until Alfred had felt that he would fall from sheer exhaustion. But finally, the greater numbers of the Anglo-Saxon army had paid off. Guthrum had fled back to his stronghold at Chippenham with a few men, leaving his army in disarray. Now, camped outside the gates of Guthrum's fortress, all Alfred had to do was wait for him to surrender. With little food and few supporters, he couldn't hold out for long.

*After a two-week **siege**, Guthrum surrendered. Alfred and Guthrum came to a peace agreement — Guthrum would leave Wessex and return to East Anglia. He and his men would also be baptised as Christians.*

ALFRED LET OUT A DEEP BREATH as he watched Guthrum's army march away. Over the past few months, Alfred and Guthrum had come to know and respect one another. Still, Alfred knew he would sleep easier with Guthrum out of his kingdom.

Turning for home, Alfred frowned. He had dealt with one Viking threat, but he knew it wouldn't be the last. The current defence system simply wasn't effective — the Viking raids were like lightning, and the fyrds couldn't be assembled quickly enough to see them off. Deaf to the happy chatter around him, he began to picture a new Wessex, one that would be safe from attack forever.

When Alfred came back to power, Wessex was in a bad way — the farmers had been too busy fighting to work their fields, the Vikings had destroyed the churches and monasteries, trade and education were non-existent, and the few laws were largely ignored.

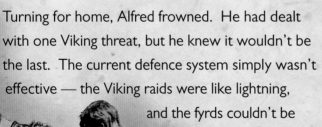

Guthrum surrenders his spear to Alfred.

Defending the Realm

AUGUST 881 Riding through his kingdom, Alfred sat tall in his saddle and gazed around with pleasure. The formerly overgrown fields were well-tended, and it looked like the harvest would be good this year. The churches were being rebuilt, trade was brisk and money was starting to flow into the kingdom again.

Alfred raised his hand to shield his eyes from the low evening sun, and gazed at the hill ahead. He could just make out a team of men, working like a colony of ants. They were building a **burh**, a fort which could be easily defended. This burh was just one of a network that would cover the whole of Wessex, making it secure against attack.

As well as building burhs, Alfred replaced the fyrds (villagers who were called on to fight when needed) with a permanent army who could react quickly to attack.

How to Construct a Burh

1. First, choose your location. Hills and harbours are ideal because they offer a clear view of approaching enemies. It should be no more than forty miles (two days' march) from another burh.

2. Dig a ditch right around the site of the burh. It should be at least as deep as a man is tall, and two to three times as wide as it is deep.

3. Inside the circle formed by the ditch, use the excavated earth to build a high earthen bank, or rampart. Cover the rampart with turf for added stability. Leave a gap in the rampart to act as an entrance. This will create a weakness in the wall — fortify it by building a strong gatehouse.

4. Build a wooden wall (a revetment) along the outside wall of the rampart. This will help to strengthen the rampart and prevent it from collapsing. The vertical face will also make it harder for enemies to attack.

5. Drive sharpened stakes into the top of the rampart. This is known as a palisade, and will make it harder for attackers to enter the burh.

6. Construct a platform around the inside wall of the palisade. From here, defenders can throw rocks and spears, or fire arrows at attackers.

7. Lastly, build the houses, foodstores and **armouries** that are needed inside the burh.

The Age of Enlightenment

NOVEMBER 887 Alfred paused in the doorway of the schoolroom and smiled. Several small heads were bent over their work. Alfred's own sons were there, with a number of other children, noble and **low-born**.

Closing the door on this happy scene, he frowned at the three grey-bearded judges who gazed at him sullenly. For months Alfred had pressed these men to learn to read, and for months they had refused.

> *"you have enjoyed the office and status of wise men, yet you have neglected the study and application of wisdom."*

When Alfred came to the throne, most people were illiterate. Alfred was eager to change that — he set up schools, employed the best scholars he could find to teach children, and insisted that anyone in a position of power learnt to read and write.

Alfred knew he had to be firm. These men couldn't do their jobs properly unless they could read. With a sigh, he offered them a choice: they could learn to read and write, or they could give up their jobs and power. The judges goggled at him, open-mouthed like fish. The eldest started to stutter an excuse, but it tailed off as Alfred stared the man down. Scowling, the three men bowed and scurried away to learn their alphabet.

Alfred rolled his shoulders to ease the tension in them, then summoned his best Latin scholar, Asser. Alfred was determined to learn Latin so that he could begin the massive task of translating all the books of law, history, philosophy and religion into English. He dreamt that one day, anyone would be able to read these books and learn from the knowledge and wisdom of their writers.

In 9th century Europe, almost all important books were written in Latin. This meant that only a few people could read them. Translating them was a huge job — there were no printing presses, so everything had to be copied out by hand.

Entering the room, Asser set a teetering pile of books on the table. Opening the top one, Alfred ran his finger along the line of Latin and began to translate haltingly. "They have eyes... but they, er, they see not."

The End of Summer

OCTOBER 890 Alfred strolled along the clifftop, relishing the feel of the autumn sunshine on his face before the bitter winter ahead. He paused to watch a team of villagers cutting wheat and expertly tying it into bundles.

For twelve years, ever since Guthrum's defeat, the Vikings had stayed in the eastern and northern kingdoms, and Wessex had enjoyed peace. Alfred had gained land in Mercia, and he was proud of the new, united kingdom he was creating — it was well-defended and prosperous, the schools were thriving and the people were happy.

Returning to his castle, Alfred was greeted by a messenger. He hopped from one foot to the other, waiting to deliver his news.

There were different groups of Vikings in eastern England, and throughout Europe. While Guthrum was alive he ruled all the Vikings in England and made sure they honoured the peace treaty with Alfred.

"Sire," he began, as soon as he saw Alfred, "I bring bad tidings. Guthrum is dead, and **Danelaw** is without a ruler."

Alfred groaned. Guthrum had been a good **ally** — strong enough to defend Danelaw from rival Viking groups from elsewhere in Europe, but sufficiently under Alfred's control that he didn't pose a threat to the rest of England. With Guthrum's death, the fragile peace between the Vikings and the Anglo-Saxons would be shattered.

Alfred knew that it was only a matter of time before the Vikings invaded. Gazing through the castle gates to the bountiful fields beyond, he vowed to keep his kingdom safe.

This picture shows Anglo-Saxon peasants harvesting wheat.

23

Battening Down the Hatches

OCTOBER 892 Alfred listened grimly as his scout gave him news of more Viking attacks in Kent.

"Three hundred and thirty Viking ships have landed," the scout reported, "and it's not just men in them this time. They've brought their wives and children too — they definitely mean to stay."

Alfred dismissed him, leaned back in his chair and rubbed his eyes. So far his new military system had worked as he had planned — his soldiers were able to respond quickly to attacks, and the burhs gave them the provisions and shelter they needed. But the Vikings were attacking from all directions now. Once again, Alfred's people were under threat. Unless Alfred could find a way to drive the Vikings out once and for all, the peaceful, flourishing kingdom that he had worked so hard to achieve would be no more.

The burhs generally worked well against Viking attack, but some of them weren't finished or properly defended, and were easily overcome by the Viking raiders.

THREE YEARS LATER Alfred stood on the ramparts of his new fortress and watched the straggling line of Vikings gallop away. He had seen off plenty of Viking raids over the past three years, but this group had been a real threat. They had sailed up the River Lea and set up camp on the border of Wessex. Alfred had puzzled for days over how to get rid of them, yet when the idea came he was amazed by its simplicity. All he had to do was block the river to prevent them leaving, so they had to either surrender or run, forfeiting their precious ships.

Alfred stretched. Calling for his horse, he and his army galloped after the fleeing invaders.

Alfred also built ships based on Roman warships, like this one. These were larger and faster than the Viking ships, so they could intercept any future Viking invasions.

© Vintage Images / Alamy

The Vanquish of the Vikings

MAY 896 Stony faced, Alfred scrutinised the Viking men who stood in front of him. They had terrorised the south coast, plundering settlements and killing anyone who resisted them. But Alfred's new navy had done its job — the Viking ships had been captured or driven off. Alfred knew that he had to send a strong message to the Vikings: he would not tolerate more raids.

"For years you have menaced my land. As pirates, you are sentenced to death. This is the fate that awaits the remaining Viking people unless they leave my kingdom."

By 896, Alfred ruled a large kingdom (see above). He called this new kingdom Englaland, which eventually became England.

TWO MONTHS LATER Alfred watched the last of the Viking ships crawl away. Their vast fleet had been reduced to just five ships. The Vikings were defeated. England was safe.

How England Was Won

Alfred drove the Vikings out of his kingdom and established a new country. So how did he succeed in ending the Viking threat when his ancestors had failed?

Alfred witnessed many Viking raids. He noticed that the Vikings avoided battle — instead they carried out rapid raids on undefended settlements, then fled before the Anglo-Saxon army could respond. Alfred established a network of forts across the whole kingdom — his burhs. From here, lookouts could spot Viking raiders, so the army could respond quickly.

Many previous kings had one large army that could only be in one place at any time. The Vikings could easily skirt round a single large army, and therefore avoid fighting. Alfred chose instead to have lots of small armies spread across Wessex. Wherever the Vikings went they were pursued by the army, so they couldn't settle anywhere.

A third reason for Alfred's success was his ships. In the past, Vikings had often attacked coastal settlements. By building ships that were larger and faster than the Viking ships, Alfred was able to prevent Viking invaders from reaching land.

Finally, Alfred made sure he had strong support from other kingdoms. He married a princess from Mercia and forged alliances with Wales and Flanders (northwest Belgium). This meant that he could rely on other countries to help him fight the Vikings.

In the end, it was so hard for the Vikings to gain land in England that they had to leave.

Divining the Future

OCTOBER 899 Edward, Alfred's eldest son, knelt by his father's bedside. He had promised Alfred that he would be strong, but a lonely tear crept down his cheek as he placed the still-warm hand tenderly on the motionless chest.

Swallowing a sob, Edward pondered his future. Could he hold on to the land that his father had fought so hard for? Could he maintain England's peace and prosperity? Could he carry on Alfred's dream of a wise and just England?

Reaching down to straighten Alfred's cloak, Edward paused. In death Alfred's stern features had relaxed and he looked younger, more carefree. The weight that pressed on Edward's heart lifted, and he was filled with a new resolve. With one last look at his father, he turned to leave the room, to face his new subjects for the first time.

Edward's fears were unfounded. Within thirty years the Vikings would be driven from Danelaw, and England united under a single king — Edward's son Athelstan (Ath-ul-stan). Even today, the royal family are direct descendants of Alfred.

Glossary

ally — A person or group of people who are on your side

Anglo-Saxons — The descendants of people who came from continental Europe and settled in Britain in the fifth and sixth centuries

armouries — Places where weapons and armour are stored

burh — A town or settlement that has strong defences

Danelaw — The area of eastern and northern England that was ruled by the Vikings.

jubilee — A celebration of an anniversary

low-born — Born to common people (that is, not nobles)

peace treaty — An agreement between enemies to end the fighting

siege — When an army surrounds a town or castle so supplies can't get through

Twelfth Night — The evening of 5th January, the end of Christmas

King John

"A misunderstood ruler?"

written by Claire Boulter

19ᵀᴴ OCTOBER 1216 John groaned as a sharp pain stabbed through his stomach. Despite the assurances of his **physician**, he knew that he didn't have long to live. Images of his past raced through his fevered mind. Once again he heard the crowds cheering as his brother Richard, tall and handsome, rode away to war. He saw again his advisors' deep bows when they learned that Richard was dead and John was king. He saw the rage on the faces of the noblemen as he told them he needed more money. Last, and most vivid, he saw his young son's pale face fading into the distance as John rode to war to protect his crown.

As a fresh wave of pain broke across his body, the furious faces of the noblemen pushed to the front of his mind again. Had they done this? Had they found a way to tamper with his food or drink to get him out of the way once and for all?

As John drew his last breath, a single thought consumed him: with England in the grip of a war over who should rule, would his son ever be king, or was this the end of his family's reign?

John probably died of dysentery (dis-en-tree) — a disease caught by eating infected food or drinking dirty water — but there were rumours that he had been poisoned.

John is buried in Worcester (Wuss-ter) Cathedral. His tomb has a marble carving of his body on it.

Family and Frustration

OCTOBER 1174 Perched on the windowsill of his room, six-year-old Prince John eased back the wooden shutter and peered curiously at the courtyard below. He recognised the man who had just arrived, mounted on a huge **charger** and surrounded by knights. He had met him several times before at feasts and celebrations. It was his father.

John only had hazy recollections of his parents. His earliest memories were of the draughty abbey he had been sent to when he was one. That was the only home he had known until a year ago, when he had been sent to live with his eldest brother, Henry.

On the whole John was happy living with Henry — he had learned to hunt and plan battles, which he loved. But despite this, he was frustrated. His sole desire was to be king, but as the youngest of seven children, four of them boys, he knew there was little chance that this would ever happen.

To make matters worse, whenever his father saw him he would ruffle his hair, roar with laughter and call him 'John Lackland'. Unlike his brothers, John had no land and no power.

Although he didn't know it, that was about to change.

In the twelfth century, England, western France and eastern Ireland were all ruled by the King of England. This area was called the Angevin (On-juh-van) Empire.

Medieval law stated that when the king died, his eldest son inherited the crown. When he died, it passed to his eldest son, and so on. If the king died childless, there could be a war over who would be king.

Fontevrault (Fon-tev-roe) Abbey in western France, where John spent the first years of his life.

A Change in Fortune

TWO AND A HALF YEARS had passed since John's father, King Henry, had visited him. Over that time, the king had awarded John more and more land, titles and money.

Alone in his chamber, John smiled to himself as he thought about how things had changed. Carefully, he took the letter his father had given him from his pocket. He knew it by heart, but he began to read anyway.

In 1173, John's brothers rebelled against their father, King Henry, to get more power. The king won the war, and decided to give John more power instead.

Dear John,

I give you these lands because, of all my sons, you alone have remained true to me. Govern them well and greater riches may follow. As you are still young, I will assist you, but it is vital that you understand your new responsibilities.

The land I have given you is yours to do with as you wish. As you know, it is usual to grant areas of land to noblemen in return for their loyalty and support, as well as the taxes they pay. The men you grant land to must have strong armies, and therefore be able to help you repel invasion. Even more importantly, you must be able to trust each of them completely, because treachery could spell the end of your rule and your life.

A good ruler looks after his subjects, from the lowest peasant to the highest baron. You should keep them safe from attack and impose laws to ensure they are treated fairly. Travel widely and see as many of your subjects as you can, because the more they see of you, the more they will trust you. If you can earn their trust and respect, they will work the land, pay their taxes and fight for you.

As well as protecting your people and lands from invasion, try to gain new territory, and thereby make our empire greater. You have been prepared for battle, and you must be at the forefront of every fight, in order to win your subjects' respect.

Finally, you must develop close alliances with other rulers so that they will support you if your land is invaded. Equally, you must be ruthless — if your best friend or your closest relative betrays you, you must be prepared to condemn him to death, so that others learn that they cannot profit from treachery.

Your affectionate father, Henry

The Path to the Throne

JULY 1189 John started as a knock came at the door. His most senior advisor entered the room, his face grave. Since the deaths of two of his older brothers, Henry in 1183 and Geoffrey in 1186, John was second in line to the throne. People had started to treat him with a respect that he enjoyed, but distrusted.

"Sire," the man began, bowing deeply, "I have news. Your father, King Henry, is dead. As you know, your brother Richard was heir to the throne. He will now be crowned King."

John dismissed him, his mind a jumble of conflicting emotions. His father and Richard had fought constantly over the past years. John had hoped that his father would make him heir to the throne instead of Richard, but now that would never happen.

Something else troubled John too. Days earlier, he had sided with Richard, knowing that their father did not have long to live. King Henry's words on learning of this betrayal rose unbidden in his mind, as they had so often over the past few days.

Richard didn't want to wait for his father's death to be crowned King. He attacked King Henry and tried to take the throne by force.

"I care no longer for myself or for anything else in the world."

Could his actions have contributed to his father's death? Shaking his head, John reminded himself that his father had been an old, ill man. The thought that now only Richard stood between him and the throne was enough to dispel the last of John's gloom.

Richard's coronation procession, painted in the 15th century.

© Hilary Morgan / Alamy

MARCH 1194 John slammed the door of his room and, fists clenched, paced the floor. For four long years Richard had been away on **crusade**. Four years during which his subjects had idealised him, built an image of him as a brave, handsome hero. Four years during which John had constantly longed to be king. As the years had passed, it had seemed more and more unlikely that Richard would return. But now he had.

John knew that he would make a better king than Richard. He had done everything he could to take the throne while Richard was away. He had encouraged the barons' hatred of William Longchamp, the man Richard had left in charge, who took more and more money from the barons to fund his own lavish lifestyle. John had even started rumours that Richard was dead, hoping that the barons would support his claim to the throne.

But now Richard was back, and all of John's hard work would count for nothing.

EARLY APRIL 1199 The last five years had passed slowly. John had been made to grovel to Richard, to beg his pardon and prove that he was loyal. Richard's patronising pardon, designed to put John in his place, angered him.

"You are only a child who has had evil counsellors"

John was out riding when the news came. Hearing the thunder of hooves behind him, he turned in time to see a breathless baron bearing down on him. William de Braose (Bray-oze) dropped from his saddle and bowed deeply.

"Sire," he began, struggling to catch his breath, "Momentous news. Your brother Richard is dead. A wound inflicted by a crossbow bolt festered, poisoning his blood."

The baron kept talking, but John was no longer listening. Richard was dead: he almost didn't dare to believe it. At long last, after years of hoping and praying, after countless attempts to gain power and secure the throne, it was finally his. At long, long last, John was king.

Richard was hit by a crossbow bolt while laying siege to a castle in France. This painting shows him on his deathbed, pardoning the archer who shot him.

© iStockphoto.com/duncan1890

A Question of Power

LATE APRIL 1199 John had hoped that, finally, his path to the throne was clear. But he had reckoned without his nephew, Arthur — the only son of his older brother Geoffrey.

The Fight for the Throne Gets Serious

As the contest for the crown heats up, we assess the candidates.

Both are direct descendants of King Henry II, but which of them should be king?

The late King Richard named Arthur as his heir in 1191. However, on his deathbed Richard changed his mind and named John as his successor.

At thirty-two, John has proven himself to be an able warrior and politician. In contrast, at just twelve,

Are we poised for war?

Arthur lacks any experience of ruling a country.

John has the support of the nobles in England and Normandy, who feel that Arthur, who has never been to England, can't possibly understand

the country's needs. On the other hand, John is disliked throughout much of the Angevin Empire, and the people of Brittany and Anjou (On-joo) favour Arthur as their ruler.

— **Breaking news** —
In a new twist, King Philip of France, who previously backed John, has switched his support to Arthur.

With both sides certain that their claim is the best, only time will tell who will win the crown.

FOUR YEARS LATER John scowled as he walked the castle's passages, noticing the furtive glances. He had captured Arthur and imprisoned him here at Rouen (Roo-on), but Arthur hadn't been seen for months, and people were getting suspicious. John paused, hearing a loud squabble in the courtyard below.

"Everyone *knows* that John murdered Arthur," the first voice shouted. "He needed him out of the way, so he killed him and threw his body in the river."

"Nah, you've got it all wrong," the second voice protested. "Arfur was tryin' to escape from 'is window, and he slipped and fell. The poor lad was swept away by the river."

John's frown deepened. Rumours that he had killed Arthur would make him unpopular. Worse still, King Philip was determined to take John's lands in France. Philip's armies were growing stronger; if John lost any more support he might lose the crown altogether.

Hope and Despair

SPRING 1204 Weary but satisfied, John leaned back in his chair. The last year had been exhausting — although nobody knew what had become of Arthur, lots of John's supporters had switched their **allegiance** to Philip, and John had lost land in France. But his most vital castles hadn't fallen, Normandy was still under his control and he knew he could reclaim the land he had lost. John reflected on the money he had persuaded the English barons to give him — with it, he would expand his army and take back his French territories.

Medieval kings were judged by how much land they won or lost during their reign. England and Normandy had been ruled by one king since 1066, so by losing Normandy John was seen as a failure.

At that moment a servant entered the room, eyes downcast. He handed John a letter and backed quickly out of the door. John tore off the seal and scanned the letter's contents. He stood, but his legs were suddenly too weak to support his weight and he sank back into his chair. John's remaining castles had fallen to Philip. Normandy was lost.

MARCH 1208 For the past four years, John's sole aim had been to win back the lands he had lost. This seemed more important than ever now that he had a son. Little Henry had been born last autumn; John had been taken aback by the overwhelming surge of love he had felt for this tiny, helpless person. He swore then that, whatever the cost, he would reclaim Henry's inheritance.

The trouble was, John thought forlornly, as his horse trudged along yet another featureless, muddy road, that the cost was so high. He needed huge sums of money to pay for new boats and more soldiers, but he knew that the noblemen were angry about the taxes he demanded of them. As well as the financial cost, John had to spend his time tramping round the country, raising money and support, when he just wanted to be at home with his beautiful wife and baby son. Shaking off these gloomy thoughts, John reminded himself that he was doing all this for them.

John married Isabella of Angoulême (On-goo-lem) in 1200. They had five children — two boys and three girls.

The Clouds Gather

JULY 1214 John drummed his fingers on the windowsill of his room in the castle at La Rochelle (Rosh-ell), scarcely aware of the sullen clouds massing on the horizon. The past years had gone well for him, and he had reclaimed some of his former lands in France. Now though, it seemed that his success might be short-lived — his supporters had deserted him and he was waiting for news from Normandy in the north, where his allies had invaded and were currently fighting Philip.

He spun round as the door opened and a limping, mud-spattered knight entered.

"Sire," the knight said, his face grave, "We, your allies, met King Philip's army in battle on the boggy plain outside Bouvines (Boo-veen). We fought bravely, unhorsing Philip and driving back his forces for a time. However, Philip's **cavalry** was strong, and attacked the centre of our army. Some of our men fled and our defence collapsed. A handful of us escaped, but I am sorry to tell you that your most powerful allies were captured and the battle was lost."

Dismissing the man, John sank to his knees. After everything he had won and lost, defeat still caused a raw ache in his chest. He knew that his chance of reclaiming the rest of his lost lands was gone, and the only option was to negotiate peace with Philip.

But he had promised the English barons victory in exchange for their support. Now that he had failed, would they still accept him as king?

Philip's horsemen were better trained than the allied cavalry, and were able to defeat them.

Stirrings of Rebellion

A YEAR HAD PASSED since John's defeat. He had lost his French territories, and a great deal of money in the process. As he had feared, the noblemen he relied on to help him run the country and pay him taxes were angry and were preparing to rebel.

John slept with a sword beside him, and jumped at every sudden noise. Rubbing his tired eyes, he drew a crumpled piece of paper from his pocket and reread the letter that his spies had intercepted.

John had demanded huge taxes from the barons to cover his war in France. They were angry that, despite taking so much money, he had still lost.

Most Honoured Lord,

We beg your help to rid England of the vile, unlawful and dangerous plague that is King John.

During his reign, he has created new taxes, and increased the amount and frequency of the old ones many times without our consent. Many of us are crippled by debt. Many of us can no longer afford to live. Many of us have no choice but to watch our estates go to ruin. Does that sound fair to you?

Those who cannot meet the king's outrageous demands face inhuman treatment, and only a few brave souls have dared to challenge the fiend. William de Braose, once a great friend of the King, refused to pay the extortionate sum demanded of him. In return, John imprisoned his wife and eldest son, who starved to death in captivity. Does this sound like the action of a just and noble man?

Although you have sworn loyalty to John, you must know that such an immoral man would not hesitate to abuse such a pledge if he saw advantage in doing so. We therefore plead with you to break your oath and come to our aid in cleansing our country of this monstrous and terrible tyrant.

We are, sir, your faithful servants.

The Swiftly Turning Tide

The document that the barons produced eventually became the Magna Carta (Latin for 'Great Charter'). This limited the power of the king, and gave his subjects rights that they hadn't had before.

JUNE 1215 John scowled and twisted his seal between his fingers. Ranged around him were the rebel barons, their looks varying from hope to suspicion to outright hostility. He looked again at the document in front of him, which listed the rebels' sixty-three demands. He was happy to agree to some of them — for example that people wouldn't be punished without a fair trial or arrested without cause.

"No free man shall be seized or imprisoned... except by... the law of the land."

But they wanted him to agree not to raise taxes without the barons' permission, and that they could seize his possessions if he broke the rules! These conditions troubled John deeply.

Knowing that he had no choice, John pressed his seal into the molten wax, making the document official. A collective sigh ran around the assembled barons as, one by one, they bowed their heads and promised to support him.

SIX MONTHS after John and the barons had reached their agreement, the fighting was more intense than ever. Neither John nor the barons had kept their side of the agreement, and the barons had started to gather soldiers and weapons — it was clear that they were preparing for war. John knew he had no choice but to force the rebel fortresses to surrender.

Some versions of the legend of Robin Hood claim that Robin lived around this time. They show him as a nobleman, deprived of his lands by John.

"I should have known that peace would never last," John thought grimly to himself, as he watched the town of Berwick devoured by fire. He had seen too many English towns burn over the past months, as he and his army marched northwards, putting enemy fortresses under siege.

John had met with more success than he could have hoped for. One by one, the rebel fortresses had fallen. The tide had finally turned in John's favour.

EARLY OCTOBER 1216 Head down, John rode onward towards yet another battle, brooding on the past few months. The war with the barons had swung both ways — one day he felt certain of victory, the next of defeat. For the past few days he had been suffering from sickness and stomach cramps, and all he really wanted to do was rest.

John's dismal thoughts were interrupted by a shout from the baggage wagons behind him. Snapped back to the present, he realised that his horse was struggling. Looking wildly around, he saw that the incoming tide had turned the estuary they were crossing to **quicksand**. He urged his horse forward and, with a mighty heave, it dragged itself clear of the hungry, sucking mud. He watched, powerless, as his soldiers and the wagons carrying supplies foundered in the deepening water. One by one, fighting desperately to free themselves, they disappeared from view beneath the waves.

Generations of treasure hunters have scoured the area where the Crown Jewels were lost, but they have never been found.

With a howl, John realised that it was not only his men and supplies that were gone, but the Crown Jewels. The crown of England was lost; John just hoped this wasn't an omen.

16ᵀᴴ OCTOBER 1216 John knew that he could do no more to secure the throne for his son. His illness had worsened over the past week and he was in constant pain. Knowing he didn't have long left, he called a trusted advisor to him and began to dictate his will.

"render assistance to my sons for the recovery and defence of their inheritance... "

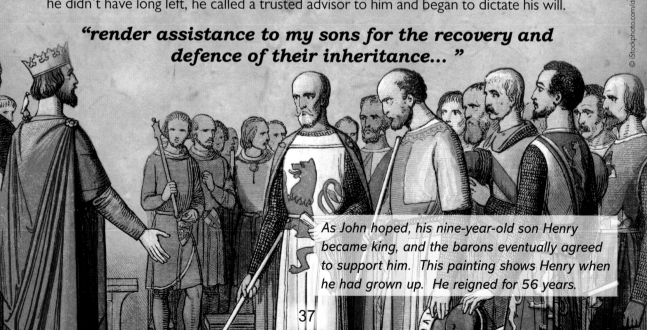

As John hoped, his nine-year-old son Henry became king, and the barons eventually agreed to support him. This painting shows Henry when he had grown up. He reigned for 56 years.

© iStockphoto.com/duncan1890

The Man and the Myth

John has had a lot of criticism over the years — he's often known as 'Bad King John', 'John Lackland' or 'John Softsword'. From a spotty, snivelling teenager to a cowardly, thumb-sucking lion, John has been depicted in lots of works of fiction over the years.

THE MAN WE LOVE TO HATE

Whether in a story, film or play, writers and directors rarely show John in a good light.

A Novel Approach

Sir Walter Scott's novel 'Ivanhoe' is set in the 1190s, when King Richard is on crusade.

Scott presents John as a weak but power-hungry man who plots to keep his brother imprisoned so he can be king.

THE SILVER SCREEN

The story of Robin Hood, the outlaw who stole from the rich to give to the poor, has fascinated children for centuries. In many of these stories, Prince John is one of Robin's main enemies.

In the Disney® film of 1973, John is a money-loving lion who sucks his thumb when he's angry or scared. He constantly swindles money out of his subjects, but Robin Hood robs him and gives the money back to the people John has taxed.

In the Disney® cartoon John is a weak and greedy prince.

© AP archive / Alamy

TREADING THE BOARDS

In the 1590s, Shakespeare wrote a play called 'The Life and Death of King John'. He shows John's nephew Arthur as the true heir to the throne, and John as a weak, deceitful character who pretends to be a strong ruler. In Shakespeare's version, John loses the support of the nobles when he orders Arthur's murder.

Much later, James Goldman wrote a play called 'The Lion in Winter', which was made into a film in 1968 and again in 2003. It's set in 1183, when John is sixteen. He's portrayed as a spoilt, sulky teenager. When his father suggests to a girl that she might marry John she says, "He's got pimples, and he smells of compost."

It's not all bad though — around 1538, John Bale wrote a play called 'Kynge Johan', which showed John as a hero fighting against the Catholic Church.

In this scene from the Shakespeare play, Arthur begs his jailer not to kill him.

©Lebrecht Music and Arts Photo Library / Alamy

So was John really a pathetic wimp who drove England to the brink of ruin, or a hero who fought to protect his country? Or might he, in fact, just have been an unlucky man who did his best under difficult circumstances? We may never know.

Glossary

allegiance — Loyalty to a nation or ruler

cavalry — Soldiers who fight on horseback

charger — A horse that is specially trained for battle

crusades — Religious wars between Christians and Muslims in the 11th to 13th centuries

physician — A doctor

quicksand — Deep, wet sand that people and heavy objects sink into

Queen Victoria

"The first diamond Jubilee Queen"

written by Holly Poynton

28ᵀᴴ JUNE 1831 Twelve-year-old Princess Victoria looked down at the history book that her **governess**, Baroness Lehzen (Lay-zern), had placed in front of her. Victoria was confused; her lessons were over for the day, but curiosity got the better of her. She opened the book, and a sheet of paper almost slipped out.

"What is this?" asked Victoria, "This wasn't in the book before..." the Princess trailed off as she studied the piece of paper more intently. On the page was a family tree, *her* family tree, showing the **order of succession**.

"Oh!" Victoria gasped, as she traced down the lines to find her name. "I am a little bit closer to the throne than I thought I was." The Baroness smiled politely.

"Indeed, Princess. You are **heiress** (air-ess) to the throne and next in line to rule Great Britain."

Victoria cocked her head to the side and thought for a minute.

"I will be a good Queen," she said. "For I know that although there is great splendour in being a monarch, there is also great difficulty."

Queen Victoria's first name was actually Alexandrina, and when she was growing up she was known as "Drina".

King William IV was Victoria's uncle. She was next in line to the throne because all of his children had died in infancy.

This is Kensington Palace, where Victoria spent most of her childhood.

A Gilded Cage

NOVEMBER 1834 Victoria sighed as she looked at the piece of paper in front of her. It was her timetable for the following day, and it was as strict and regimented as ever.

She was supervised every moment of every day. She wasn't allowed any time alone, and she even had to hold her mother's hand when she walked down a flight of stairs. Throughout the day, her tutors and governess would watch her every move, and then at night, she would sleep in the same room as her mother. Visits from other children were few and far between. It was a very cheerless existence.

"Thank goodness I have you!" Victoria exclaimed as she patted the head of her spaniel, Dash. The dog licked her hand as she turned her attention back to the piece of paper.

7 am: Your lady's maid will wake you and your mother. You shall rise, and your maid will help you wash and dress.

8.30 am: Descend to the dining room for breakfast, accompanied by your mother.

9.30 am: Proceed to the sitting room with your mother, where you will continue your needlepoint under the supervision of Baroness Lehzen.

11 am: Make your way to the schoolroom. Mr Steward will arrive to tutor you in writing and arithmetic. Mr Davys will relieve Mr Steward at 12 noon, and instruct you in Geography and Natural History.

1.30 pm: Accompany the Baroness to the dining room, where luncheon will be served.

3 pm: Return to the schoolroom, where Monsieur Grandineau will tutor you in French.

4 pm: Accompany your mother for a stroll around the gardens. Your maid will provide you with a shawl, cloak and mittens.

5 pm: Return to the sitting room, where you are permitted an hour of recreation under the supervision of Baroness Lehzen.

6 pm: Retire to your chambers with your maid, and dress for dinner.

7 pm: Accompany your mother to the dining room for dinner.

After dinner, you will retire to your chamber along with your mother, and your maid will help you dress for bed. Say your prayers before the candles are extinguished.

A Royal Awakening

20ᵀᴴ JUNE 1837 Victoria stirred as she heard a gentle tap at her bedroom door. She ignored it and tried to go back to sleep. Now she was 18 she finally had her own bedroom, and she relished her newfound privacy. There it was again. This time it was followed by her mother's voice, speaking in a hushed but desperate tone.

"Victoria, wake up. The Archbishop of Canterbury and Lord Conyngham are here to see you. It is of the utmost urgency." These words jolted Victoria awake. She reached for her dressing gown and wrapped it around herself hurriedly.

Victoria entered her sitting room, where the morning sun was just beginning to sneak through the window and creep onto the carpets. Her heart was pounding in her chest, but she tried to remain calm and composed as the two men were shown into the room.

The men fell to their knees as soon as they caught sight of her.

"Your Majesty," Lord Conyngham began, "it is with great sadness that I inform you that your uncle, King William, passed away at 12 minutes past 2 this morning. Consequently, you are now Queen."

The men continued to talk, but Victoria's mind began to whirl. She knew she would face difficulties during the early days of her reign, not least because she was female and only 18 years of age. However, she was determined to fulfil her duty to her country, to be a noble sovereign who was caring, courageous and who earned the love of her subjects.

If King William had passed away before Victoria's 18th birthday, her mother would have ruled on Victoria's behalf until Victoria was old enough to rule.

This painting shows Victoria receiving the news that she had become Queen.

The Dawning of a New Era

28TH JUNE 1838 Victoria trembled as she sat on the throne in Westminster Abbey. The cavernous building was filled with noblemen from across the globe, and every noise echoed solemnly around the lofty ceiling.

Victoria stared ahead as the Archbishop of Canterbury neared her side. The moment had finally arrived: she was to be crowned Queen of Great Britain. As she felt the weight of the crown press down on her brow, the trumpets blared and the ceremonial guns fired. Victoria swore to herself that she would remember this moment forever.

Victoria's coronation attracted an estimated 400 000 spectators, lasted five and a half hours and cost around £6 million in today's money.

One by one, nobles approached her throne to pay their respects by touching the crown and kissing her hand. Lord Rolle, an elderly gentleman who was dwarfed by his heavy ceremonial robes, shuffled up the steps to greet her. Without warning he stumbled and fell. The congregation gave a collective gasp as he hit the floor with a thump. Time stood still as those nearby hesitated, unsure of the right way to act.

Unfazed, Victoria rose from her throne, walked serenely down the steps and helped Lord Rolle to his feet, allowing him to pay his respects without mounting the stairs again. She smiled at him and clasped his hand warmly. He bowed as deeply as he could, grateful for her small act of kindness.

With the coronation complete, Victoria walked down the nave of the Abbey towards the ornate doors. As she stepped outside, the sunlight flashed brilliantly off her bejewelled crown, casting a spectrum of colours across her smiling face. The crowds of well-wishers launched into a deafening cheer, rejoicing at the first glimpse of their newly crowned queen.

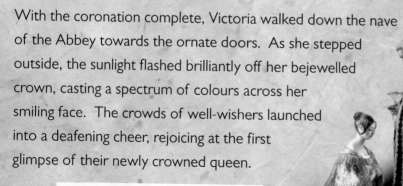

*Victoria receives the **sacrament** during her coronation.*

To Have and To Hold

OCTOBER 1839 Victoria admired the emerald ring on her hand. She had been wearing it for several days now, and every time she glanced at it, it made her heart sing.

The ring had been given to her by her fiancé, Prince Albert. The couple had met for only the second time last week, but the butterflies in Victoria's stomach told her that she had found more than just a husband.

Victoria inhaled deeply as she sniffed the wedding bouquet that had been placed in front of her. Her wedding was only four months away, and every day a stream of flustered servants presented her with menus or decorations for approval. Although everyone else thought four months was too little time to prepare for such an important wedding, Victoria felt the time stretched before her like an eternity. As well as making Victoria and Albert husband and wife, the wedding would free Victoria from her mother's watchful eye and give her the independence she craved.

Even though Victoria was Queen, her mother still insisted on living with her at Buckingham Palace. Victoria resented her mother because of her part in Victoria's strict upbringing.

Victoria wore a white dress when she married Albert — this started a tradition of brides wearing white. Prior to this, there was no single colour associated with wedding dresses.

10TH FEBRUARY 1840 Row upon row of spectators lined the streets of London as Queen Victoria and her new husband drove away from the chapel at St James' Palace. The chilly winter drizzle hadn't dampened anyone's spirits, and the cheers echoed in Victoria's ears long after her adoring subjects were out of sight.

Little did Victoria know that this adoration wasn't shared by everyone, and that some of her subjects wanted to end her reign once and for all.

Victoria in her wedding dress.

A Dance With Death

30TH MAY 1842 "I am quite well!" Victoria exclaimed to the concerned servants and advisors who clustered around her. "But I do believe I need to rest!"

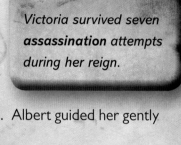

*Victoria survived seven **assassination** attempts during her reign.*

Prince Albert took his wife by the hand, and led her to her private sitting room. As soon as they were out of view, Victoria's body sagged and she leant heavily on her husband. Albert guided her gently to a sofa and knelt by her side, clasping her shaking hand.

"You are the bravest woman I know," he said tenderly. "We were foolish to even attempt it. You could easily have died tonight."

Victoria raised her chin slightly, "If that murderous fiend hadn't been apprehended tonight, then we would have lived our lives in fear. A Queen should fear nobody!"

Arrest Report *30th day of May 18 42* **Metropolitan Police**

John Francis **was charged with** _high treason_

POLICE COMMISSIONER'S OFFICE 1842

Arresting officer(s): _PC Ernest Davies_

Report: *On the evening of the 29th May 1842, Her Majesty, Queen Victoria, and Prince Albert were riding in an open-top carriage along The Mall to Buckingham Palace. The assailant, John Francis, approached the carriage and pointed a pistol at Her Majesty. The gun did not fire. Police were called to the scene and a search was conducted to locate Francis, but his whereabouts were not discovered.*

The following evening, 30th May 1842, Her Majesty suggested following the same route as before in the hope of luring out Francis. A large number of plain-clothed policemen were positioned along the route to protect Her Majesty. As before, John Francis approached the carriage and shot at Her Majesty, but he was apprehended by officers and placed under arrest.

Signed:

An Exhibition Fit For a Queen

1ST MAY 1851 The day dawned glorious and bright, just as Victoria had hoped it would. Today, she and her family were going to open the Great Exhibition, an enormous exhibit of wonders from around the world.

The exhibition was the result of several years' hard work by Prince Albert — he had been in charge of creating and organising the event. Victoria's heart swelled with pride as they neared Hyde Park: she knew that her husband had worked so hard to make his dream a reality.

As her carriage turned the corner, she caught sight of the exhibition building for the first time. The blue sky was reflected a thousand times over in the polished panes of glass, and the steel frame glinted in the midday sun.

A jubilant crowd of eager visitors had already gathered in Hyde Park, and the hum of excited voices drifted through the warm spring air. As the throng of people caught sight of their Queen, they began clapping and cheering, waving flags, handkerchiefs and hats.

Victoria's cheeks flushed when she saw their earnest welcome, and she felt exceptionally privileged to be the guest of honour at such a momentous occasion.

The Great Exhibition was open between May and October 1851. It is estimated that it attracted over six million visitors.

© iStockphoto.com /ixer

The Crystal Palace was made from 300 000 panes of glass, and the interior was the size of five football pitches.

"This day is one of the greatest and most glorious of our lives... It is a day which makes my heart swell with thankfulness."

Queen Victoria and her family at the opening of the Great Exhibition in 1851.

29TH MAY 1851 Victoria smiled as her son, nine-year-old Prince Bertie, gazed from side to side, his eyes as big as saucers. Every inch of the Great Exhibition had something to delight the senses. Here: the playful toot of steam engines, the whirring of cogs, the flash of electric sparks. Over there: the glitter of gold, the sparkle of gems and the opulence of marble. Everywhere: the heady scent of melted chocolate and heavenly perfume.

COME TO THE GREAT EXHIBITION

By appointment to Her Majesty, Queen Victoria

Wondrous things from the WILD WEST, the Far East and everywhere in between.

GLORIOUS GEMSTONES

Be awed by the magnificent Koh-i-Noor diamond, all the way from mysterious India!

Exquisite Artworks

Delight in hundreds of tapestries, paintings and sculptures from across the globe!

MARVELLOUS MACHINERY

Try out Great Britain's astounding hydraulic press. Lift 1144 tons by yourself!

100 000 EXHIBITS WAITING TO BE DISCOVERED!

EXOTIC CREATURES

Dare you approach the humongous elephant?

Steam Engines

Witness the future of British power before anyone else!

AT THE CRYSTAL PALACE HYDE PARK

Celebrate Man's Greatest Achievements!

Pain and Progress

MARCH 1853 "Your Majesty, I must advise you against this!" exclaimed the royal advisor fretfully, but the Queen merely dismissed him with a flick of her hand.

For weeks now, all she had heard was pompous old men telling her what to do, but it was of little use — her mind was already made up. Ever since Albert had mentioned Dr Snow's pioneering work with **chloroform** (claw-ro-form), she had wondered whether it could alleviate her suffering during childbirth. Now she was heavily pregnant with her eighth child, she had arranged for Dr Snow to administer the **anaesthetic** (an-es-thet-ic) during the delivery.

Her advisors were very much against the use of chloroform: there had been some cases where its use had led to the patient's death. But Victoria was unwilling to take advice from anyone who hadn't endured the pain of childbirth first-hand.

A famous case used to highlight the dangers of chloroform was that of Hannah Greener, who supposedly died from a chloroform overdose while having a toenail removed.

APRIL 1853 Victoria cradled her newborn son in her arms and wrapped his blanket a little tighter.

The delivery, and the chloroform, had been a success, and Victoria had nothing but good things to say about the anaesthetic.

"...the effect was soothing, quieting and delightful beyond measure"

She sighed and stroked her son's cheek. If only other expectant mothers would follow her example, then much of the unpleasantness surrounding childbirth could be reduced.

Queen Victoria, Prince Albert and some of their children.

The Darkness Descends

AUGUST 1859 "What's wrong, my dear?" asked Victoria, her brow furrowed in concern, as another low moan escaped Albert's lips.

"It's probably nothing," replied Albert through clenched teeth, his body bent slightly in attempt to ease the cramping in his stomach, "but I think I'll go to bed early and try to get a good night's sleep." He gave his wife a quick bow as he left the room, barely masking a wince as another wave of pain surged through his stomach.

Victoria shuddered as the candles near her flickered. It was as if the angel of death had flown over the Palace.

14ᵀᴴ DECEMBER 1861 Although Prince Albert's room was filled with people, there was a deathly silence. Victoria sat at his bedside, her face obscured from view as she pressed her pale cheek on to his cold hand, which lay on the blanket.

Five of their nine children, usually so boisterous and playful, sat quietly around his bed. The only sound that could be heard was an occasional stifled sob and the ticking of a clock.

Prince Albert had died that evening. **Typhoid** (Tie-foyd) fever had been the doctor's diagnosis, but Victoria didn't care what had killed him, only that he had been snatched away from her too soon. Victoria barely noticed as dusk fell and, one by one, the others left the room.

Queen Victoria was so distraught by Albert's death that she wore black for the rest of her life.

*For many years it was thought that Albert died of typhoid, but modern historians think that it might have actually been cancer or **Crohn's** disease.*

*Albert was laid to rest in this **mausoleum** (more-sel-lee-um) at Frogmore House in Berkshire.*

49

A Golden Year

21ST JUNE 1887 More than twenty-five years had passed since Albert's death, and even though today was a day of celebration, Victoria still felt his absence keenly. Her procession through London wouldn't be quite the same without his reassuring presence by her side. Despite her sadness, Victoria tried not to dampen the mood. Royals, nobles and ambassadors had travelled from every corner of the British Empire to celebrate her Golden Jubilee, and it was her duty as Queen to be an accommodating and dignified host.

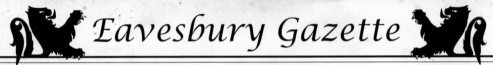

Eavesbury Gazette

SATURDAY, JUNE 25 1887   ONE PENNY

THE JUBILEE CELEBRATIONS

THIS WEEK marked fifty years since Queen Victoria took the throne, and festivities have been held up and down the country.

Royal Celebrations

Her Majesty attended a royal banquet at Buckingham Palace on the 20th June, along with fifty foreign kings and princes.

The following morning, she travelled in an open-top carriage around the streets of London accompanied by an escort of Indian cavalry and dozens of troops of soldiers.

After the procession, the Queen appeared on the balcony of Buckingham Palace to wave to the general public. She later attended another feast and watched a firework display from the palace gardens.

The Children's Jubilee

It was not just the Queen who enjoyed the festivities. Approximately 30 000 lucky children attended a Children's Jubilee in Hyde Park on 23rd June.

Before leaving, each child was presented with a Jubilee beaker, and one lucky girl received hers

Florence Dunn receives her beaker from Her Majesty.

directly from the Queen.

Outside of London

The celebrations were not confined to the capital. Towns up and down the country organised their own processions and parades.

The Jubilee events were a complete success which were enjoyed by thousands, and they have encouraged a sense of national pride.

An Ever-Shrinking World

JULY 1887 Victoria gazed at the map before her. She traced her finger over some of the territories under British rule: Canada, Australia, New Zealand, Hong Kong. It was said that the sun never set on the British Empire.

Under Victoria, the British Empire expanded. At its peak, the Empire covered 14 million square miles.

Her finger lingered over India: the jewel in her crown. Recently she had been given the title 'Empress of India', and although she hadn't visited this mysterious land, she couldn't help but wonder about its splendid sights and customs.

Victoria couldn't visit India herself — the difficult sea journey would take several months, and she couldn't be away from Britain for that long — so she was determined to bring India to her.

FEBRUARY 1888 "Excellent, Your Majesty!" beamed Abdul as he bent over her work.

The Queen glowed with pride. She had been learning **Hindustani** for the past few months, and although she had struggled with the unfamiliar characters to begin with, she was finally beginning to see results. Abdul had joined her household staff from India, and he was an excellent teacher.

"I have taken the liberty of preparing a surprise for Your Majesty." Abdul said, barely masking a smile.

"A surprise? For me?" Victoria was in her seventies, but surprises still filled her with childish glee.

"Indeed, madam! I have requested that your chefs prepare an Indian dish for your dinner this evening. A delicious curry made to my family's own recipe!"

Victoria clapped her hands in delight. "I am very much looking forward to tasting it."

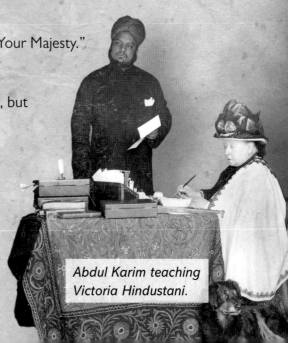

Abdul Karim teaching Victoria Hindustani.

The End of an Era

2ND FEBRUARY 1901 Throngs of onlookers crowded up and down the streets of London, but this time there was no cheering, no waving and no jostling. All that could be heard was the steady march of approaching footsteps and the mournful firing of the gun salute.

Victoria's devoted public had always come out in droves to show their support, and today was no different. Dressed in black, they hung their heads in silence and braved the freezing conditions to say farewell to their Queen.

As the coffin passed by, a few delicate flakes of snow began to fall from the leaden sky. The crowds stood in silent vigil as the clatter of hooves on the icy cobbles faded away.

Queen Victoria died on the 22nd January 1901 — she was 81 years old. She died at Osborne House on the Isle of Wight surrounded by her family.

Glossary

anaesthetic — A drug that causes a temporary loss of sensation

assassination — The act of murdering an important figure

chloroform — A liquid that used to be used as an anaesthetic

Crohn's disease — A disease of the digestive system

governess — A woman who teaches the children of a wealthy household

heiress — A female who will inherit her parents' power and fortune

Hindustani — A language spoken in parts of India

mausoleum — A large tomb

order of succession — The sequence of people who are in line to the throne

sacrament — A Christian rite where members of the congregation are given wine and bread to represent the blood and body of Jesus

typhoid — A disease carried in dirty water

AHR21